THE
HERETIC'S GUIDE
TO VEGAN COOKERY

ANDY MURRAY

Published by The Good Elf Press

Text copyright © 2008 by Andy Murray
The moral right of the author
has been asserted.

Author photographs by Kim von Coels-
kimvoncoels@hotmail.com

Vegetables and fruit illustrations© Faye
Chadburn-
www.fayesuzannahchadburn.blogspot.com

All other photographs and drawings by the
author.

   ISBN number 978-0-9560868-0-8

The views expressed in The Heretic's Guide to
Vegan Cookery are the author's alone and it
should not be inferred that anyone else
mentioned in the book or indeed, not
mentioned in the book necessarily shares
them.
For those not laughing, the author would like
to state that he realises that irreverent teasing
always comes from an unhappy place and is
an outward sign of his own inner spiritual
dysfunction. He would like to take this
opportunity to suggest that perhaps he should
be felt sorry for, rather than beaten to death
with a talking stick or religious artefact.

Andy can be contacted by email-
thehereticsguide@yahoo.co.uk

Contents

Introduction

The Recipe Dinosaurs   1

Bloody Good Food   2

Cooking with Glastonbury   3

Johnny Depp Wrestling in Mud   4

Cold Leek and Potato Soup   6

Presentation Through Intelligent Design   7

Mouthfeel   8

Perusing the Cookbook Shelf   9

Missing Something?   11

Things You Might Find Useful   12

Soups

Basic Stock   18

Jerusalem Artichoke Soup   19

Roasted Tomato and Fresh Coriander Soup   26

Green Split Pea and Mint Soup   27

Armenian Lentil and Apricot Soup   28

Sweet Potato, Fennel and Tarragon Soup   29

Ukrainian Borscht   32

Malaysian Tofu and Pineapple Soup   33

Austrian Leek and Potato Soup   34

French Farmhouse Soup   35

Scotch Broth   37

Red Pepper and Sweetcorn Chowder   38

Nettle Soup   39

Spiced Moroccan Chickpea Soup   41

Roasted Pumpkin and Garlic Soup   44

Bolivian Peanut Soup   45

Tom Kha Hed (Thai Galangal and Mushroom Soup)   46

Raw Soups

Sylvie's Spanish Gazpacho   48

Celery and Cashew Soup   49

Tomato and Red Pepper Soup   50

Raw Sweetcorn and Red Pepper Chowder   52

Raw Nettle Soup   53

Salads

Roasted Cauliflower, Pecan and Radicchio Salad   56

Carrot and Arame Salad   57

Moroccan Couscous Salad   58

Herby Rice Salad   61

Rocket and Baby Spinach Salad   62

Malaysian Cucumber and Pineapple Salad   63

Zanna's Coconut and Potato Salad   64

Bean sprout Salad Japanese style   68

Tabbouleh   69

Dips

Hummus   72

Moroccan Spiced Carrot Dip   73

Teradot   77

Butterbean, Brazil Nut and Cumin Dip   78

Baba Ganoush   79

The Great Outdoors

The Great Outdoors   82

Useful Ingredients to Swipe   83

Wild Food   85

Wild Plant Information   86

Playing with Fire   92

Burning and Cooking   93

Ukrainian Borscht

I love this soup. You could always grow your own through the spring and summer. They're incredibly easy- quick to mature and not prone to pests or anything really.

And it's raw beetroot or nothing for this soup. Don't be tempted by the cooked and vacuum-packed beetroot. The colour and taste the raw beetroot gives to the soup as it cooks is a necessary part of the finished soup. And the texture's never quite the same either with the pre-cooked ones. And anyway, it's just wrong.

Instructions

2 onions, finely chopped

4 large, uncooked beetroots, peeled, julienned and cut into short lengths

2 carrots, julienned and cut into short lengths

1 medium potato, diced

3 tomatoes

2 tbsp red wine vinegar

4 cups stock

3 tbsp chopped fresh dill

¼ medium white cabbage, shredded and cut into short lengths

Salt and pepper

A swirl of vegan cream (optional)

Fry the onions on a medium heat until soft.

Add the beetroot, carrots and potato.

Skin the tomatoes by soaking in boiling water for thirty seconds and peeling then finely chop and add to the vegetables with the vinegar, stock and half of the dill.

Cook for about three quarters of an hour or until the beetroot is tender.

Add the cabbage and cook for a further ten minutes or until the cabbage is softening.

Add the rest of the dill and salt and pepper to taste.

Serve with rye bread.

Malaysian Tofu and Pineapple Soup

I grow Vietnamese coriander (*Persicaria odorata*) in my herb garden where it romps away, quite unaware of being in the wrong country. It's an essential ingredient in Malaysian cooking. If you can't buy it or grow it, substitute coriander.

  Galangal is crisper than ginger and a little harder to chop. Buying it dried is a passable option if you soak it for a few minutes before using. As a last resort, substitute ginger. Though I must say that the smell and taste of fresh galangal is worth the hunt.

  Malaysians use herbs in salad quantities and the soup reflects this so don't be alarmed. It's also pretty much a meal by itself and perfectly happy being a main meal as well as soup. So that's nice.

Instructions

½ block/113g/4oz plain fresh tofu

2 onions, finely chopped

1 inch galangal, finely sliced and cut into tiny short matchsticks

1 garlic clove, minced

1 red bird's eye chilli, finely diagonally sliced

2 medium carrots and 2 sticks of celery, julienned and cut into 1 inch lengths

5 de-stalked and sliced Shiitake mushrooms

2 cans chopped tomatoes

2 fresh tomatoes, roughly chopped

1½ cups diced pineapple

½ tbsp chopped fresh mint

1 heaped tbsp chopped fresh lemon verbena

2 heaped tbsp chopped fresh oregano

10 finely chopped leaves Vietnamese coriander

½ cup bean sprouts

1 tbsp fresh lime juice

1 tsp toasted sesame oil

Salt

Cut the block of tofu into small cubes and deep fry until the cubes begin to turn golden and lift to the top of the oil. Remove from the oil and drain on a kitchen towel. Set aside.

Fry the onions, galangal and garlic on a low heat until soft.

Add the chilli, carrots, celery and mushrooms and continue frying for a few minutes before adding the can of tomatoes, the fresh tomatoes and pineapple.

Add about half a cup of water initially and simmer until the vegetables are softening.

Stir in the herbs, bean sprouts, lime juice, sesame oil and season to taste. If the soup is too thick, add a little more water.

Serve immediately.

Red Pepper and Sweetcorn Chowder

Another no frills, straight forward, very tasty soup. There are so many variants on this classic recipe too, but this is the rough feeling of the one that I do. A lot of recipes keep the main part of the soup unblended but I prefer it kind of smooth. If you are able to use fresh sweetcorn, just scrape the uncooked kernels off the cob with a knife before using. Frozen is pretty good too, or tinned sweetcorn as a last resort. Make sure they're sugar and salt free though. Adding a dessert spoon of peanut butter to the soup at the end works very well too if you fancy and it's still in keeping with the feeling of the soup.

Instructions

2 onions, roughly chopped

½ red chilli, roughly chopped

2 red peppers, roughly chopped

2 celery sticks, roughly chopped

3 medium potatoes, peeled and roughly chopped

3 fresh sweetcorn cobs or 2 cups frozen sweetcorn

4 cups stock

Salt and pepper

3 tbsp of vegan cream (optional)

Fry the onions on a low heat until browning, then add the chilli, peppers, celery, potatoes and the fresh or unfrozen sweetcorn. Gently sauté until the vegetables are softening.

Add the stock and simmer for another five minutes before hand-blending.

Add more water to the soup if it's too thick.

Salt and pepper to taste.

Stir in the vegan cream if so desired.

Serve.

Nettle Soup

This is a very lovely, very British soup. Obviously a wonderful spring soup, but with judicious cutting back of nettle plants every month, you'll have a fresh new supply for most of the year. If you don't have a nettle patch, then let one happen in an unused part of your garden. If you don't have a garden, then get out somewhere away from roads, traffic and chemical spraying, and pick there instead.

Get a medium sized bowl and a carrier bag. You'll just be taking the top few leaves of the new growth, before they flower. Use washing up rubber gloves and a sharp knife and gather into one hand before putting into a bowl and then off-loading into the bag. It's a boring, often irritatingly painful job, so either persuade someone else to do it for you, or do it very, very quickly before the repetitive tedium and nettle stings turn you insane. Stop when you've got a good half filled carrier bag.

Treat like fresh spinach. Rinse thoroughly in a bowl of cold water still in your rubber gloves, before lifting out the nettles into a pan. There's usually lots of critters left behind in the water so take the bowl outside and set the water and the myriad of insect, arachnid and possibly crustacean life free. They will thank you with little bug hugs.

If you fancy more of an Irish feel then omit the creamed coconut and after frying the onions, add half a cup of fine oatmeal and continue frying briefly until golden. Then continue with the recipe and you've got a soup pretty close to a very ancient Irish soup called Brotchan Neanntog.

Instructions

2 onions

2 medium potatoes, roughly chopped

5 cups stock

½ courgette, roughly chopped

A carrier bag ½ full of fresh nettles

1 inch creamed coconut

¼ tsp ground nutmeg

Salt and pepper

Fry the onions on a low heat until soft then add the potatoes with the stock. Simmer until soft, adding in the courgette towards the end of cooking.

Let the nettles cook down in a separate pan for a few minutes just in the rinsing water left on the leaves. The leaves should still be bright green but reduced in volume with softened stalks. You could just cook the nettles straight in with the potatoes and stock but I like the extra control so that I know the nettles aren't over-cooking and losing their colour.

Add the cooked nettles, creamed coconut and nutmeg to the soup and hand-blend. Season.

Roasted Pumpkin and Garlic Soup

The classic autumn soup, or my take on it anyway. This soup is thick and satisfying, with the garlic giving an extra spiked dimension to the satiny sweetness. I find pumpkin to be a bit boring and tasteless as it is, so roasting is a necessary bit of business. You can always substitute a squash for the pumpkin.

Instructions

1 medium pumpkin

2 onions, roughly chopped

3 garlic cloves, finely chopped

1 potato, peeled and roughly chopped

4 cups stock

1 tsp ground ginger

1 tsp poppy seeds

Salt and pepper

Chop up the pumpkin into halves, then quarters using a small serrated knife to poke through the tough skin and follow around. A large knife can too easily slip.

Gouge out the seeds and the dark orange strands behind them.

Cut each quarter into eighths if they're still too large. The skin can then be easily pared off with a knife by laying each segment on its side and slicing off bits in succession. It's the easiest, safest and most efficient way to prepare pumpkins and squashes I've found so far.

Chop into medium chunks and roast in a 170ºC oven until the pieces are halved in size and soft all the way through. Some caramelisation is good but not too much as this will affect the colour of the finished soup.

Meanwhile, fry the onions on a low heat until transparent.

Fry the garlic separately until golden. Don't let it brown. Add into the soup.

Add the potato to the onions and the stock. Cook until soft.

Add the ginger, poppy seeds and the roasted pumpkin. Try to avoid transferring too much fat from the roasting dish into the soup.

Hand-blend with your hand set to its blade attachment.

Salt and pepper to taste.

Bolivian Peanut Soup

Remember when using fresh chillies that the seeds are the hottest part, followed by the part nearest the stalk so you can always scrape away the seeds or use a little less chilli if unsure about the heat. To find out how hot your tiddly little chilli is, an evil chef's tip is to gently rub an itchy eye with a finger, just after chopping one.

   The soup can then be partially processed with one eye closed in agonising pain if a smoother soup is required.

Instructions

1 onion, roughly chopped

1 fresh red chilli, finely chopped

2 medium potatoes, peeled and finely diced

3 carrots, finely diced

5 cups stock

½ cup fresh garden peas

6 tomatoes, skinned and roughly chopped

3 tbsp peanut butter or ½ cup plain raw peanuts ground in food processor

Salt and pepper

1 tbsp chopped fresh coriander

Fry the onions on a medium heat until browning then add the chilli, frying on for a minute or so.

Add the potatoes and carrots and sauté until the vegetables are softening.

Add in the stock, peas, tomatoes and the peanut butter or ground peanuts and allow to simmer for five minutes.

If the soup is too liquid, add a little more peanut butter.

Salt and pepper to taste.

Just before serving, stir in the chopped coriander.

Tom Kha Hed (Thai Galangal and Mushroom Soup)

Oh my god, oh my god! Quickly! Get the ingredients! This is without doubt one of the best soups I've ever tasted. Just exquisite.

Shiitake mushrooms work well with this soup too but if using, remove the stems as they are usually a bit too fibrous.

Instructions

1½ inches fresh galangal, peeled

3 stems lemongrass

1 red bird's eye chilli

3 kaffir lime leaves (dried is ok)

3 spring onions

2 tomatoes, roughly chopped

10 fresh oyster mushrooms, thinly sliced

¼ medium cauliflower, separated into small florets

½ red pepper, thinly sliced then halved

2 tins coconut milk

1 tsp rice vinegar

Up to 1 cup of water

Salt and white pepper

1 tbsp fresh lime juice

Finely, finely slice the galangal then cut into very thin, very short matchsticks.

At an angle, very finely slice the white parts of the lemongrass into long ovals (discard the green ends) and do the same with the chilli.

In a medium sized pan, add the galangal, lemongrass, chilli, kaffir lime leaves, half a tin of coconut milk and half a cup of water and boil for five minutes.

Chop the spring onions into short lengths, cutting at an angle like the chilli and lemongrass just to be fancy.

Add the spring onions to the pan with the tomatoes, mushrooms, cauliflower, red pepper, the remaining coconut milk, rice vinegar and enough of the remaining half cup of water to leave the soup with some substance. Use your judgement.

Allow to simmer on for quarter of an hour until the vegetables are softening but still retaining a bright colour.

Salt and pepper to taste and squeeze in the lime just before serving.

Raw Soups

These are surprisingly good. Gazpacho is an authentic recipe, the others are just the kind of soups I do for the raw food people that I get not to cook for. They work well enough to be acceptable for anyone, actually. They're also a damn good way to eat loads of raw vegetables quickly.

If you're still stuck in meat heaven but feel the need for a quick health fix hell, or just bound up in the occasional heat of an English summer when you can't be bothered with cooking, then these really are dead useful. If the thought of cold soup sends shivers up and down your spine, then call it a smoothie or something.

Once again, if you can use organic vegetables and good extra virgin oils, so much the better. The difference is noticeable. Also, these soups will only do two or three people each. If you need more, they will double up, triple up, dance, do magic tricks and take your photo.

Sylvie's Spanish Gazpacho

Though my friend Sylvie strenuously denies that this is a raw soup, it so is. Gazpacho has to be based on good ingredients. So, proper, ripe vine tomatoes, cold pressed extra virgin olive oil and so on. Don't skimp.

Instructions

6 tomatoes

½ cucumber, roughly chopped

½ green pepper, roughly chopped

1 garlic clove

1 tbsp white wine vinegar

1 tbsp olive oil

Salt

3 ice cubes

Plunge the tomatoes into boiling water for thirty seconds, then remove and discard the skins.

Now roughly blend all the ingredients and serve immediately.

If you're not all the way raw then eat with a decent ciabatta or similar for full greatness.

Celery and Cashew Soup

To make the celery a little more acceptable in raw soup, make a shallow cut in the back at the top of each stick of celery and peel away and down from the cut. This should take away the strings of fibres with it, meaning you'll have a smoother soup at the end.

Instructions

¼ cup cashews, soaked for ½ hour

1 spring onion, roughly chopped

5 celery sticks, roughly chopped

½ avocado

1 tbsp white wine (optional)

2 tsp sesame oil

1 tbsp fresh lemon juice

Salt

This is really too easy.

Bung all the ingredients into a food processor and whizz up with some water.

If you want it smoother still then finish off with a hand blender.

I seem to have stopped typing.

Is this the end of the recipe?

It seems a bit short.

Add salt.

Tomato and Red Pepper Soup

Instructions

1 large red pepper

5 ripe tomatoes

1 tbsp chopped red onion

3 sun-dried tomatoes, soaked and drained

½ cucumber, peeled

2 tbsp chopped fresh basil leaves

1 tbsp fresh lemon juice

1 tsp olive oil

Salt and pepper

Roughly chop all the ingredients apart from the runny ones and put everything into a food processor.

Whizz up, adding some water if needed.

Strain through a sieve if you prefer.

Season. Whichever one you like but summer's quite nice.

Going Round in Circles

What could be more beautiful and evocative of the New Age than the mysterious formations that appear every summer in the fields across south-west England? More complex and artful as each new day dawns, the crop circle* is a wonder of the modern world, defying all attempts by the Scientific Community to furnish a logical explanation other than the most obvious. Everyone else knows that aliens make them.

Amazingly, the very formation of crop circles changes the plants inside the circle in a magical and sub-molecular way, but it's something that only happens if you really really believe, because intent changes stuff. It's amazing anyway and grain taken from the centre of crop circles can even be ground into flour or planted where it will germinate and grow into another plant. Amazing but true.

Crop circles are distinctly lacking around Glastonbury unfortunately, due to a tragic Catch-22 situation. If a farmer was ever able to grow even one field of wheat or oil-seed rape nearby, the aliens could finally nip in and create a special circle for newcomer locals, desperate for their years of believing to be acknowledged. But because of the many extreme allergies and pollen hyper-sensitivity experienced by the Glastonbury population, this has up to now sadly proven impossible.

As consolation, they hold a yearly crop-circle conference instead, where photographs of the phenomenon can be studied in safety, without sneezing.

Only good aliens make crop circles. Evil aliens lack the necessary opposable thumbs to adequately push rollers and unwind balls of string which at least makes the crop circle's hidden message to all human beings a little more straight forward. The last thing fragile minded people need would be to receive an order to mutilate cattle and take over the world, amid the crop-coded pleas for world cuddling. **

The collective term for crop circles is a calendar.

**Thanks single-handedly to David Icke, a mystical footballer, THE FACTS about these bad and evil Royal Family-loving aliens are now in the public arena. His web site also carefully exposes the other LIES spread by the RULING ELITE, giving us the tools to break free of their control. Icke is merciless in his pursuit of THE TRUTH and provides an invaluable resource for anyone wishing to write in STRESSED CAPITALS, increase their ability to hear voices and prove at last that people really are following them, possibly the Men in White.*

Zanna's Coconut and Potato Salad

This is a real moreish potato salad. Coconut and potato are such a good marriage and both love chilli. It's my take on a salad my friend Zanna made once. I loved it so went away and got my version near to it I think.

Instructions

20 cut to bite size new potatoes

½ fresh red chilli, finely chopped

2 spring onions, finely chopped

1 tin coconut milk

½ tsp ground coriander

2 tsp ground cumin

½ tsp turmeric

½ tsp kolonji

½ cup roughly chopped fresh coriander

Salt

Slightly salt the water before cooking the potatoes. When ready, drain and cool.

Fry the chilli briefly until changing colour before adding it and the rest of the ingredients apart from the fresh coriander into the potatoes.

Leave to sit for half an hour so the potatoes absorb some of the flavours.

Add the chopped fresh coriander and salt to taste before serving.

Signs and Designs

One day in 1925, a woman living in Chilton Polden called Katharine Maltwood found that she could see shapes on a local map that looked just like Guinevere and Arthur Pendragon. Not only that, but the two forms she kept on trying to get other people to see definitely formed part of a much larger zodiac, a forgotten spiritual gift to mankind from the Ancients.

Defined by ancient tracks, field boundaries and streams, Maltwood's zodiac spread across the landscape of the Vale of Avalon, a Star-Temple echoing the astrological signs up above in the night sky and she was to be its guardian. It soon became known as the Glastonbury Zodiac.

I would like you to join me as I try to re-enact her process.

Just for fun, I'm doing away with the map idea and instead, I'll be going up the Tor and looking out over the landscape for real. This is potentially very exciting. Perhaps the Ancients have left more mystical signs coded below our very feet that only I can read, making me very special. Let's find out.

I meditate for couple of minutes, half way up on a bench in the sun to attune myself to the hidden thingummy whatsits.

My mind's blank now and I'm screwing up and squinting my eyes as I begin to walk... up, up, up... I've squished something on the path but my eyes are by now too attuned to see what it is...

I'm nearly at the top now, a bit... out... of breath... and I'm looking around, looking around... crouching a little distance from the Djembe players and... now. I'm linked.

I'm contemplating a whole load of fields that I can feel intuitively are suggesting the shape of a spiritual figure. It's becoming clearer as I'm looking at it. I'm wondering if it's Jesus and whether it's a veiled reference to the messianic bloodline. Actually, now I'm looking at it a bit longer, it could be a headless eagle brandishing its own noggin in its claw... Then again it could be a horsey, or a baa-lamb... or maybe a simulacrum of my Mum or the sign for Aquarius. Damn it. It could be anything. Um... Maybe those fields over there might be more productive... Dot to dot, star to star and hedge to hedge. It's not as easy as Mrs Maltwood made it look. It's an exhausting business, this kind of thing.

Using the basic zodiac, astrology has been used from time immemorial to divine the future, give clues to present problems and explain the past. It's still the only way to truly decide whether someone is to be trusted, enjoyed as a friend, arrested or married.

Astrology is an amazing tool to run your life by, without having to waste time with the fraudulent pseudo-scientific mumbo-jumbo of Science. Astrology explains wars, thunderstorms and plague. We can even use it historically. For example, if we know exactly when and where Queen Elizabeth the first was born, we can find out exactly who she really was, without having to waste time on often fictitious history books. With it we can even discover why Einstein was so damn clever.

Astrology is way better than sex.

However, let's not forget that for every Einstein with his perfect trines, there is a Hitler sporting bad conjunctions and evil planetary alignments. Some believe that we need to be honest with ourselves and grasp the nettle. Without those meddlesome stars and planets controlling and changing our lives, they argue, wouldn't we all have a bit more of a fighting chance at true happiness? If we could destroy them all, maybe with laser beams or nuclear bombs, then we could be truly free. Well, until that happy day, we can at least console ourselves with the fact that we're not Capricorns.

The Great Outdoors

Attention!

And now, attention please.

I promised myself that if I ever wrote a cookbook, I would have some stuff about camping, cooking and being outside. It was a big part of my summer life and there's still something unbeatable about food cooked on a fire in the middle of nowhere. So here is some of the stuff I wish I'd known twenty years ago. While tongues should still be kept firmly in cheeks for the next chapter, all the information is genuine. I won't be joking about the basics of plant identification and the skills used in enjoying wild resources, either while camping or just exploring the natural world. Just so you know. Everything else is subject to my whims and opinions and might need a friend's tongue to help out.

Wild Plant Information

Chickweed (*Stellaria media*) is an extremely common plant/garden weed all year round even when most other plants have succumbed to winter. It makes a good salad ingredient and is also useful as a pot herb. It can be briefly fried or added to a stew towards the end of cooking taking the place of spinach.

Wild Garlic (*Allium ursinum*) is a very useful onion/garlic flavoured plant, growing from early spring into early summer. Use the leaves, flowers or seeds raw or in stews and stir-fries. Bear in mind that the leaves are mild compared to the flowers which are mild compared to the seeds.

Nettle (*Urtica dioica*) and **Dandelion** (*Taraxacum officinale*) are readily available everywhere, all the year round if you're lucky, though the main spurt of new growth is in spring. The new leaves are packed full of nutrients. Good raw or cooked. Dandelion buds can be briefly fried up in quantity. They're a nice mix of bitter and sweet. Nettles can be eaten raw if you carefully but firmly pick and fold a leaf in two from underneath and keep folding until you have a parcel. Press down a few times, pop in your mouth and chew. You can also toast the leaves Ray Mears style by holding a long nettle stem in a campfire for a few seconds to destroy the stings and then just eat off the leaves. Otherwise, use the leaves in stews, soups, anything you like. They're great.

Alexanders (*Smyrnium olustratum*) is one of the first umbellifers to appear in spring, introduced by the Romans. Look for its shiny green leaves. Use the stems like asparagus and the unopened flower heads like cauliflower, either raw or cooked, and the seeds as a spice. A good bulky addition to the pot, though a little unusual tasting.

Pennywort (*Umbilicus rupestris)* is a great fresh salad ingredient to be found in winter and spring, with round semi-succulent leaves growing often from banks or old walls, mainly in the south-west of the country.

Wood Sorrel (*Oxalis acetosella*) has clover-like leaves and tastes like wood sorrel. Good in white sauces.

All the members of the cabbage/mustard family (*Cruciferae*) are edible, from **Lady's Smock** (*Cardamine pretensis*) to **Hairy Bittercress** (*Cardamine hirsute*) and **Shepherd's Purse** (*Capsella bursa-pastoris*). All good sources of spiciness. Think radish and nasturtium leaves. Can be added to stews or just eaten raw.

Watercress (*Nasturtium nasturtium aquaticum)* can be found throughout the year but be careful to cook before use, unless completely sure of its purity, due to the possibility of liver fluke on the leaves.

Mushrooms

Because of the obvious plethora and popularity of mushroom identification guides I'll just include my favourite mushroom and leave it at that...

The **Parasol Mushroom** *(Macrolepiota procera)* is one of the finest tasting common mushrooms, easily identifiable by its similarity to a parasol. To distinguish it from the less edible **Shaggy Parasol** (*Macrolepiota rhacodes*), check that its stalk has snake-skin like scales on it rather than being smooth and the mushroom's white flesh turns pink and not red when snapped in two.

Fruit

Fruit can be found from early summer onwards, from wild strawberries and wild raspberries to bilberries, blackberries, apples, pears, cherries and plums. The less obvious but very common fruits like rosehips, sloes and haws need a little processing first but they're worth the effort.

Nuts

Nuts are the easiest source of protein in the vegan forager's arsenal but of course they only occur for a few weeks in autumn. They consist of hazel, walnut, beechnut, sweet chestnut and acorns. Nuts are a little indigestible raw. Soaking overnight, cooking or roasting first is a very good idea.

The acorns of the **Holm Oak** (*Quercus ilex*) can sometimes be edible enough to eat as they are. They tend not to have the amounts of tannins present in the **English Oak** (*Quercus roba*) though even those acorns are edible when the tannins have been leached away by repeated soakings in water.

An up to date version of letting a river leach them, even though it sounds a little weird is to put a string bag of shelled acorns into the water flushing tank of a toilet. Every flush takes away the leached tannins and gives you fresh water for them to soak in. Otherwise, soak them in a bowl. Either way, this can take up to two weeks. Test for tannins by biting into one. The taste is bitter and astringent so if it is, back in the water until it isn't.

The acorns can now be left to dry on newspaper, then either stored or ground like coffee beans. You can use the resulting flour in recipes, either by itself or mixed in with other flours. Acorn flour might be tasteless but it's nutritious, filling and completely undervalued as a food source. The use of acorns across the world for food is covered in fascinating detail in a book called '*Oak*' by William Bryant Logan. Highly recommended.

And then there's **Pignut** (*Conopodium majus*) which really isn't a nut. It's not a nut in the same but different way that a peanut isn't a nut. It's actually the small lumpy tuber of a delicate looking umbellifer that can be found in or near open woodland. It tastes a little like chestnuts. Remember that the uprooting of the plant is illegal without the permission of a florid-faced tweedy landowner with two black Labradors. Don't get shot.

Seaweeds

And so on to seaweeds. Or algae. The two names are interchangeable, except algae is a possibly more correct definition.

Seaweeds can be divided into three groups. Red, green and brown. They aren't actually considered plants by science, rather marine multicellular benthic algae but they do exhibit similarities, with parts a little like roots, stems and leaves.

They are without doubt a fantastically nutritious and easily found resource, the best found from spring onwards. In this country there aren't any poisonous seaweeds growing by the shore and the differing species are mostly quite distinctive so the more unpalatable ones can easily be avoided. Always pick seaweed far away from any discharge pipes or fresh water outlets onto the beach, however healthy the seaweeds seem to appear. Harvesting on the low tide line is a good idea. Only take some of the living plant, leaving the holdfast (the equivalent of a root) intact so it can keep growing and always wash well before use.

There are around twelve thousand species world-wide. Red seaweeds account for nearly half.

Red Seaweeds

Dulse (*Palmeria palmata*) is a flat fronded seaweed, variable in colour from a pinkish red to a reddish purple. It's high in fibre, protein, trace elements and iron. Being an epiphyte it can often be found growing on oarweed as well as on shoreline rocks. It can be eaten as it is, dried, ground or added to stews as a flavour enhancer. It reduces like spinach when cooked, taking about half an hour. Eat with potatoes.

Carageen/**Irish Moss** (*Chondus crispus*) is a reddish brown algae. It's well known for its thickening qualities and used extensively in puddings, chocolate milk etc. Traditionally in Ireland, it's cured in damp foggy conditions for a couple of weeks which bleaches out the colour before drying in hopefully sunnier weather. Put in stews for a bit of nutritious thickness.

Purple Laver (*Porphyra laciniata or P. umbilicalis*) is the famous component in Welsh laver bread. It can be found often lying slickly over other seaweeds on exposed rocky shores. Repeatedly wash to remove sand, then cook for a few hours with a little salt until breaking up. The resulting spinach jelly-like mass can be combined with fine oatmeal and fried or as Roger Phillips suggests, spread on fried bread, though without the bacon for me. In the same family as Japanese Nori, I reckon it's best toasted in a low oven then crumbled into food, or just eaten as a snack. This is my favourite British seaweed for taste. If you want to prepare it in this way, then after washing it clean and squeezing as much water out of it as you can, let it dry out for twelve hours by spreading it all out on newspapers to allow the water to evaporate. If you can put it all outside in the sun, this'll just take a couple of hours. Then put into the oven on a low heat until crispy. It has a nutty, iodine-rich taste and children seem to adore it.

Pepper Dulse (*Osmundea pinnatifida*) is only reddish on the lower shore. On the higher shore the tiny, stubby, stiff fronds bleach out to a yellow-green due to the increased light of shallower waters. It can often be found growing en mass across rocks, covering large areas. Eat raw or use dried as a peppery spice. Its taste is distinctive and surprising good and strong for such a small seaweed.

Green Seaweeds

Sea Lettuce (*Ulva lactuca*) is, as its name suggests, very much like a limp, soggy looking lettuce. It's edible raw, though a little chewy. Chopping quite finely before eating helps. It can also be briefly fried and eaten like greens.

Gutweed (*Enteromorpha intestinalis*) is the bright green soggy grass looking seaweed that's to be found plastered to drying rocks. It's worth picking a good amount of this one. It stores a lot of sand and stone amongst the strands so wash it thoroughly before use and pat as dry as you can or let the water evaporate away before using. Good fried.

Brown Seaweeds

Oarweed (*Laminaria digitata*), is also known as kelp, in the same family as Japanese Kombu. This is traditionally put in with cooking beans as it helps to break down some of the more indigestible sugars and speeds up the cooking time. It's also great as a stock flavouring, as a vegetable, chopped into bits or roasted and ground as a condiment. Both oarweed and its relative, **Sugar Kelp** *(Laminaria saccharina)* can be cut into small squares and deep-fried.

Bladderwrack (*Fucus vesiculosus*) is the seaweed that everyone seems to recognise but hardly anyone thinks to have a nibble of it. It's a shame, because bladderwrack is best eaten fresh and raw. I promise you, it tastes as good as any Japanese sea-weed. It's free and it's incredibly common.

Posh Things to do with Vegetables

Posh Things to do with Vegetables

A curiously small chapter considering the vegan's necessary love of vegetables. Of course there's a world of things to do with them but most are just fantastic by themselves and that doesn't really justify giving them a page each, saying 'steam them'. So I'll mention a couple of my favourites here to save a bit of paper.

Cavolo Nero, the Italian black kale is amazing steamed, as is purple sprouting broccoli and Savoy cabbage.

Sweet potatoes are best baked like normal potatoes and eaten simply with salt, pepper and a little olive oil.

But when carrots are freshly pulled from the ground or garden peas podded as you walk away from the plant, who needs to cook anything anyway?

Braised Red Cabbage

Red cabbage is different and special. While other brassicas hate being over-cooked, red cabbage practically cries with joy at the prospect of a good, hard, long braising. So don't be scared. This is a slight variant of the tried and tested way to a wonderful cabbage dish. The basics are always the same though. Some sort of wine or vinegar, apples, sugar and spices and a good amount of red cabbage. So have a play.

Instructions

1 small red cabbage, de-stalked and finely shredded

1 onion, finely chopped

2 garlic cloves, minced

1 large cooking apple, cored and finely chopped

1 tbsp red wine vinegar

4 juniper berries, crushed

1 tbsp brown sugar

1 bay leaf

Salt

Combine all the ingredients with a little salt and some freshly ground black pepper and put into a baking dish.

Cover with greaseproof paper or baking parchment, with foil on top. Otherwise, the cabbage and the vinegar will react with the metal, causing ugliness in paradise and that just won't do.

In a 170ºC oven, cook covered for a good hour, up to an hour and a half, before serving.

Mashed Swede

OK. Mashed swede isn't that posh but I won't be stopped. This is simply the best thing to do with the beautiful swede. Simplicity is such a simple yet often over-looked technique and this is it pared down to its lovely essentials.

Instructions

2 medium swedes

1 tbsp olive oil

Salt and roughly ground black pepper

Peel and roughly chop the swedes.

Boil for at least twenty minutes in enough water to cover.

Drain and mash well with olive oil, a pinch of salt and a couple of pinches of black pepper.

That's it. Sublime.

Roasted Hasselback Potatoes

This is a posh way to roast normal white potatoes. Choose a floury variety like Maris Piper. The trick is to chop slices down into each potato at intervals, stopping short of a full cut. The effect is a fanning of each potato, and a shortened roasting time. It's a little seventies style but still an effective and attractive way to serve potatoes. I've never managed to get these potatoes to end up soft enough using the traditional way but I love the effect so we'll just do it a bit like normal roasties instead. Feel free to experiment though.

Instructions

16 smallish medium potatoes or as many as you think you can handle

2 chopsticks

1 bunch fresh rosemary

½ tsp paprika

2 tbsp olive oil

Salt and pepper

Peel and cut each potato in half into the normal potato roasting shape and place flat end down.

The easiest way to achieve the next part is to place a chopstick in front and behind each halved potato being chopped. Now cut down fine, regular slices across the length of the potato. Repeat for all of them.

Once all sliced, put them into a pan of water and bring to the boil. Let them boil covered for five minutes before draining them.

Place them onto an oiled baking tray and insert a few sprigs of rosemary here and there by opening some of the slits with a knife. To add more colour to the potatoes, mix half a teaspoon of paprika into some oil before brushing over the potatoes with a pastry brush.

Season with salt and pepper and roast in the oven at 180ºC for about forty minutes, periodically spooning oil back over the potatoes as they cook until the potatoes are browning and softening.

Niki's Garden Peas with Caramelised Lemon

This is a very simple but effective tweak to serving peas.

Instructions

1½ lemons, thinly sliced, halved and de-seeded

1 tbsp olive oil

2½ cups garden peas

Salt

Fry the halved slices of lemon over a very low heat until they begin to caramelise.

Turn over and repeat for another minute or so.

Boil the peas and drain before adding the lemons with a little salt to taste and putting into a serving dish.

Sprouts in Ginger and Tamari

Don't cut crosses in the bottom of sprouts before cooking them. Just as people do it without ever questioning why they do it, I shall offer no explanation why you shouldn't do it either, other than it's very silly.

   This is a recipe for when you've got a surplus of sprouts and want to do something else with them other than boil them, which personally I really like as well.

Instructions

1 tbsp peanut oil

1 onion, finely sliced

1 tbsp grated fresh ginger

30 sprouts, finely sliced

1½ tbsp tamari

1 tsp sesame oil

Heat up the oil in a pan and add the onion. On a medium heat, fry until the onion is browning.

Add the grated ginger.

Fry on for thirty seconds before adding the sprouts.

Let them fry on for about 8 minutes, stirring frequently until just tender before adding the tamari and sesame oil.

Serve immediately.

Roasted Carrots with Maple Syrup and Saffron

Roasting carrots is such a nice thing to do to them. They're so full of sugars that they can't help but caramelise in the most delightful way, helped by the maple syrup. Honey would be the normal one for this but lots of vegans don't use it. So maple syrup is a good compromise.

This works great with parsnips too, or use both together.

Instructions

12 large carrots

10 whole medium shallots, peeled

2 tbsp olive oil

4 unpeeled cloves of garlic

2 tbsp maple syrup

15 strands saffron

2 tsp celery seeds

1 tsp caraway seeds

Salt and pepper

Chopped chives for garnish

Peel the carrots if they're not organic then cut into quarters lengthways. If the carrots are particularly large then half them again. Then cut into two inch lengths. Keep the size as even as you can.

Pour a good slosh of olive oil into a baking tray and put in a pre-heated 160ºC oven for five minutes to heat up.

Add the carrots and shallots and put back in the oven for twenty minutes before taking out and adding all the other ingredients apart from the chives.

Season and mix well.

Put back in the oven for fifty minutes, occasionally stirring.

Serve with a scattering of chives.

Pineapple Pachadi

This is a lovely Kerala dish, sweet and savoury and goes well with most curries. Ideally you should use grated coconut flesh but you can use creamed coconut with a little dessicated coconut if not. To grate a coconut, crack your coconut and ease out the flesh.

  It can be easier to get out the flesh if before you crack it open, you bake the coconut in a 180ºC oven for quarter of an hour first. Peel away the thin skin with a peeler. Grate! We'll be frying in coconut oil too, chaps. This is the oil of choice in Kerala and I must say without butter ghee, it's a very good option indeed for all vegan curries.

Instructions

About ½ pineapple/2 cans pineapple

10 small shallots, peeled and roughly chopped

2 tbsp coconut oil

½ tsp ground mustard seed

1½ tsp ground cumin

1 red chilli, finely chopped

1 cup fresh grated coconut

5 curry leaves

½ tsp turmeric

2 tbsp plain vegan yogurt

2 tsp mustard seeds

Salt

Peel your pineapple and chop into little bits. Cook in a little water until pulpy. If using canned pineapple, then food process and set aside.

Fry the shallots in the coconut oil on a medium heat until softening.

Add the ground mustard seeds, cumin and chilli and fry on for a minute or so.

Add the grated coconut and fry for a few seconds to slightly brown off, before putting it all into a food processor and whizzzing up until smooth.

Add to the pineapple with the curry leaves, turmeric and yogurt and cook on a medium heat for a few minutes.

Separately fry off the mustard seeds in oil until sputtering and add to the curry.

Salt to taste.

Tassels and Red Paint

What guide would this be if you weren't shown the ancient Art of Feng Shui? It influences door colour, product placement, shop fronts and where the toilets are located in most of Glastonbury's shops.

Feng Shui is an ancient system for getting what you want, like stamping your feet or holding up a post office with a replica shot-gun except done nicely with the harmonising mystical skills of geomancy.

Chinese people six thousand years ago observed that life could be hard sometimes, what with monsoons and famines and early death. So with the desperation brought about by border-line starvation, they started to experiment, planting their rice and millet crops in different places until they grew better. After a while, they discovered that places with soil would grow better crops than places with more bare rock, like mountains. These soil-rich places became especially auspicious when combined with the added magic of nearby water and Feng Shui was born. Soon, places with lots of trees and rock-free clay were considered auspicious for building houses and digging graves while other sites with bigger, better trees, monks and a large peasant work force nearby were right energetically for building temples.

But Feng Shui finally came of age when it was realised that it could be applied indoors. Pre-Feng Shui, although the houses luckily already had corners, the doors were not painted red, pictures of nuzzling lovebirds were often noticeably lacking and the polished metal mirrors and motorised table waterfalls that would soon grace auspicious walls and corners of discerning Chinese everywhere just cluttered up the floor. With a *Kazaam!* that old Feng Shui worked its magic yet again, delivering hope for a brighter tomorrow with a much needed tidy up.

After only a hundred years of using Feng Shui, all across China, millions of people now lived a well-fed life of beauty and calm, uninterrupted by snowstorms, earthquakes, torrential rain, untimely death and anything unsettling at all. Energy flowed uninterrupted through all. Harmony had been achieved across the land with a careful appliance of Magic.

While the ancient Chinese basked in a Golden Age, the often circular accommodation of northern Europe's suffering Neolithic population meant that Feng Shui didn't really catch on there until millennia later. Even after the idea of building square cornered houses revolutionised European living, it would still have to wait for centuries out in the cold until the New Age was invented and Feng Shui finally found its Western home.

Hazelnut and Celery Risotto

This is my version of a basic risotto, tweaked for vegan taste-buds and extended to include some of my favourite ingredients. I keep going on about it, but as with most things, risottos benefit greatly from damn good ingredients. If you can, then the Carnaroli or Vialone Nano varieties are two of the best. If not, then Arborio rice can still give good results.

Instructions

1 ½ cups hazelnuts

2 onions, finely chopped

3 garlic cloves, minced

5 sticks of celery, finely sliced

2 tbsp olive oil

2 cups Carnaroli rice

2 cups dry white wine

2 pints hot stock

6 ripe, vine tomatoes, finely chopped

2 tbsp fresh marjoram, finely chopped

1 tbsp yeast flakes

Salt and freshly ground black pepper

Firstly, lightly toast the hazelnuts in a 170ºC oven. Don't let them get any further than lightly turning brown. Allow to cool a little until the bitter, papery skins can be scrunched away from the nuts and blown away.

Wrap them up in a clean tea towel and gently beat for a little bit with a rolling pin. Let the noise and adrenalin subside. If you're now sobbing uncontrollably, you've got issues and should seek outside help.

Fry the onions, garlic and celery for five minutes in olive oil on a medium heat until the onions are softening. Add the dry rice and continue frying and stirring for a minute or so before adding the wine and turning up the heat, cooking and stirring for a few minutes until absorbed. Stir.

Add the first cup of hot stock, tomatoes, marjoram and the yeast flakes and simmer on a medium heat. Stir…

Keep adding another cup of stock when the one before has been absorbed, until the rice is cooked but still retaining some bite. Don't stop stirring. This should take around quarter of an hour from the time you put in the first cup of stock. Stir.

As you near the end of cooking, lessen the amount of liquid you're pouring in. It's a skill that might take you a couple of goes to get spot on but it's worth it. The risotto is ready when the rice is creamy and plump, still retaining some bite with just a little thick creamy liquid between the grains.

Add the hazelnuts and salt and pepper to taste before leaving it to rest with a lid on for a few minutes before serving. You can stop stirring now, by the way.

Roasted Pepper and Wild Mushroom Lasagne

Well, here it is. My nil cheese, nil carne lasagne. It tastes good and it works. But it's not the real thing. What's a boy to do?

   For a vegan lasagne, one of the tricks is to get strong tastes, colours and textures into each layer, rather than worrying about how it compares to a butter/milk/cheese/meat lasagne, because it doesn't. But it's pretty damn good considering it's minus those ingredients. It'll certainly put a smile on any vegan/dairy intolerant person's face, which I suppose is another good reason to include the recipe here.

   If you want to make the recipe with wheat-free lasagne sheets, then take care. It's possible to do, but difficult to get right. Depending on the make and ingredients, the sheets might benefit from a couple of minutes soaking in hot water before assembling the lasagne proper. Some are best put in dry and allowed to stand in the completed lasagne for an hour before cooking. What you don't want is a over-chewy lasagne or a mush with no bite at all. Experiment a few times and you'll discover what works best. Just don't get your hopes up too high. Right then, here we go.

Instructions

3 red peppers

7 garlic cloves

20 button mushrooms, thinly sliced

½ cup dried wild mushrooms, soaked, drained, squeezed and finely chopped

2 red onions, finely chopped

2 cans chopped tomatoes

1 tbsp tomato purée

½ tsp smoked paprika

1 cup fresh, lightly torn basil

Salt and pepper

2 tbsp sunflower oil

1 bay leaf

½ cup white flour

2 cups hot soya milk

¼ tsp freshly ground nutmeg

1 cup brazil nuts

1 packet lasagne verdi

1½ cups vegan live yogurt

2 tbsp nutritional yeast flakes

Salt and pepper

Roast the red peppers in a 170ºC oven with a little oil for about half an hour or until the skins are blackening.

 At the same time, put the garlic cloves, complete with skins in a little parcel of tin foil with a drizzle of olive oil and put that in the oven too. They should only take twenty minutes to roast.

Remove both the peppers and garlic when ready and allow to cool a little.

Remove the seeds and skins from the peppers and chop into thin lengths. Set aside.

Fry all the mushrooms in sunflower oil on a medium heat until most of the liquid has been cooked off. Reserve.

Fry the onions on a low heat for a good quarter of an hour until caramelised.

Pop out the roasted garlic from the skins and chop up before adding to the onions with the tins of tomatoes, the tomato purée and the smoked paprika. Simmer on a low heat for twenty minutes until thickening, stirring occasionally.

Add the chopped fresh basil, salt and pepper to taste and set aside. **Cont'd...**

Roasted Pepper and Wild Mushroom Lasagne *concluded*

Make the béchamel sauce by heating the olive oil then adding the flour slowly, stirring it in. Add the bayleaf and fry in the paste for thirty seconds before introducing the soya milk slowly, again stirring to prevent lumps. When a smooth medium thick consistency has been achieved, add the fried mushrooms, nutmeg and salt and pepper to taste.

Put the brazil nuts into an electric blender or food processor and process until completely ground. Add half to the béchamel sauce and reserve the rest.

Put a thin layer of tomato sauce in the bottom of a deep baking dish and cover with lasagne sheets. Then add a thin layer of white sauce with the mushrooms, a layer of lasagne, a layer of tomato sauce, a layer of lasagne sheets, a layer of white sauce with the red peppers, a layer of lasagne and finally a layer of tomato sauce. If you can squeeze another layer of lasagne sheets in, so much the better.

To make the topping complete, mix the remaining half of the ground brazil nuts with the yogurt and the two tablespoons of nutritional yeast flakes and salt to taste. Now spread it out across the top and into the oven with the finished dish for at least half an hour on a medium heat until the lasagne is bubbling and the top is browning off.

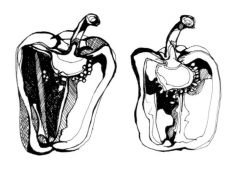

All Flesh is Grass. Discuss

"You're no better than Hitler, you lot. It's not natural. Get a life. It's people like you that cause all the wars. Vegetables scream when you pull them up so that makes you a murderer. Oh, poor little plant...
*Have a burger, hur hur hur..."**

Vegans exist in a thin scatter across society, occasionally clumping in the more alternative towns across the country. They can sometimes be found trying to live together in car-free, oil-free, herbivorous rule-filled communities or communing at a vegan festival stall eating chocolate cake.

When first hanging out with the alternative set in Glastonbury, perhaps at the Assembly Rooms, it's acceptable to be a righteous vegan, even a fruitarian. But after a few months, it just gets boring for everybody else. Vegans are then taken to one side and introduced to that most perennial of New Age obsessions, the indigenous peoples of America. Because native Americans have always eaten buffalo and worn moccasins and as they're so peaceful and wise, it must actually be OK to eat meat. Animals are just another food and clothing manufacturer provided by the universe but only if you remember to say thank you first. Then they don't mind. It's good anyway not to get stuck in one way of thinking about ethics for too long, when there is a world of equally valid angles to try. This is called relaxing your attitude.

Once-upon-a-time vegans can be spotted by subtly eaves-dropping in on conversations in Glastonbury's vegetarian cafés. The first sign that you're over-hearing an ex-vegan is when you hear words lifting out of the background noise like '... *really* lacking in energy...', or, '... I was told by my Homeopath/Kinesiologist/Acupuncturist...'. This will be said in a slow, deeply sincere and measured tone while looking intently into the other's eyes. At this point there will be a break while Native American spirit guides are discussed, before returning to the previous subject with a question about the serious ethical implications of someone reincarnating as a pig and then someone else killing and eating said pig and would that then be karmic cannibalism?

All these words are intoned while secretly chewing on a MacDonald's they've sneaked into the café in a bag. This is definitely evidence of someone who's relaxed their attitude.

For those still calling themselves vegetarians, a loop-hole exists called fish. Fish are vegetables and may be eaten, in fact, they want to be.

**All true, I'm afraid.*

127

just to leave a few lasting, living memorials to his awful strength and power. For what ever reason, each Master had had their energy shifted to resonate into frequencies destructive to pure Reiki energy, which must be an incredibly uncomfortable sensation for each of them. The three Masters have all agreed to remain for the time being behind a bank of orgone generator-enabled shields so that world-wide Reiki can continue.

Death came quickly in the end. Kwa had been under observation by the Reiki secret police for some time and becoming aware that Kwa was aware of them, they finally decided to act. Maybe they stopped him from continuing any further, but the point is moot. It is more likely that Kwa just allowed himself to be cornered, deeply confused by his power, desperate for meaning and cut through with grief.

Protected by the power of Angel Reiki, or so they thought, thirty police descended on his mother's home. Although Kwa made an attempt to break through the police's energy defences it must be admitted that it was a desultory effort. Turning back to resume gazing out over the city, he turned his energy inwards and switched off his chakras, causing his heart to arrest almost immediately. On releasing his energy in death Kwa succeeded in a final parting gesture. After having killed upwards of one hundred people, the police were to be the last taken. Unprepared perhaps for the purity of the energy hidden beneath the blackness, each face in death betrayed neither shock or horror but ecstatic wonder. Warriors accompanying a king to the underworld. That might have even surprised Bert Kwa.

Marinated Tofu

This is my favourite way to have tofu. It would be the winner of the bland awards if it wasn't for water, damn its eyes. This is the trouble with tofu and yet its saving grace. Its ability to absorb and take on flavours is exceeded only by the ability of the Borg collective to absorb absolutely everything.

   If you can get it, fresh tofu is of a better quality and less grainy than the more readily available mass produced tofu, but even the crappest tofu is ok for this.

Instructions

One 226g/8oz block fresh plain tofu

1 inch ginger, grated

2 tsp wholegrain mustard

1 fresh red chilli, finely chopped

2 garlic cloves

3 tbsp shoyu or tamari

After gently squeezing out some of the loose water from the tofu, cut the block into medium cubes and put in a bowl.

Add the ginger, mustard, chilli, garlic and soy sauce.

After a good stir, leave to marinade for at least half an hour, periodically stirring to keep the mix soaking into the tofu.

Spoon out the cubes onto a baking tray with a bit of oil and put in a 170ºC oven for about half an hour, stirring the tofu periodically to prevent the drying marinade from catching.

When the tofu has browned and firmed, take out of the oven and eat, maybe with a simple stir-fry or even as I have them, on a default setting, with roasted potatoes and steamed broccoli on rice. It's simple but very effective. Possibly curiously obscure too.

Antipasto

Antipasto is the Italian equivalent of hors d'ouvres. As a starter, it can include pretty much anything. This is my version that I really love. It has to be served with a good Italian ciabatta. Nothing else is good enough.

Instructions

1 small tin artichoke hearts, drained and quartered

2 peppers, roasted, peeled and thinly sliced

1 cup decent mixed black and green olives

½ cup sun-dried tomatoes, soaked and chopped

½ cup fresh torn basil leaves

½ cup olive oil

2 garlic cloves, minced

A few sprigs fresh oregano

A few sprigs fresh thyme

½ red chilli, minced (optional)

Salt and pepper

Well, this is going to be easy. Mix all this together and let it marinade for a bit.

Eat.

Aloo Bonda

This is just delightful. Battered, spiced mashed potato, deep-fried.

   I go to Indian restaurants a lot and occasionally, if the chef is any good, this'll start me making little noises of happiness. The first time I tasted one that I loved was at the Namaste Kerala restaurant in Southampton. It's worth the journey. Overall, they serve some of the best Keralan food around. When I got back home, desperate to unpick their technique, I tried deep frying just the spiced potato. I can report that this is a really bad idea. Here's how to actually do it. As usual, the classic Indian ginger, chilli and garlic combo come along to add substance and depth to the taste, though it works fine without. There aren't many different ways to do this and my version isn't awfully different from most other aloo bonda recipes but it's such a nice thing that here it is.

Instructions

½ tsp mustard seeds

½ tsp cumin seeds

1 onion, finely chopped

1 green chilli, minced

1 garlic clove, minced

½ inch ginger, finely grated

4 medium potatoes, boiled and lightly mashed

¼ tsp ground fenugreek

¼ tsp turmeric

1 tbsp fresh lemon juice

½ cup chopped fresh coriander

Salt

For the batter-

1½ cups gram flour

¼ tsp turmeric

¼ tsp chilli powder

½ tsp baking powder

Salt

Fry the mustard and cumin seeds until popping, then add the onion, chilli, garlic and ginger and slowly fry on a low to medium heat until the onion is browning.

In a bowl, mix the onion, mashed potato, fenugreek, turmeric, lemon juice and fresh coriander together. Salt to taste.

For the batter, mix together the dry ingredients and add water little by little, mixing as you go until you have a thickish mix. Salt to taste.

Make small golf-ball-sized shapes with the spiced potato and dip each one well into the batter with your fingers before gently placing them into a wok or pan half full of hot oil.

Deep fry briefly in batches until golden brown, not forgetting to turn them over so that they cook evenly. Allow to drain on some kitchen roll before serving.

Spinach and Potato Pakoras

Frozen spinach is incredibly useful for this recipe. Much easier than using fresh spinach. Try not to use pre-chopped frozen spinach though. It makes things a lot more difficult for this dish. It can be more like using wet green dust than spinach leaves.

If the oil is too hot, you'll end up with crunchy pakora outsides but uncooked middles. If the oil isn't hot enough, they'll turn out a bit soggy, so I would recommend getting it just right. Treat it like a baby's bath water and keep testing the temperature with your elbow. Not really. Put a small piece of bread in the oil. When the bread rises to the top of the oil, sizzling, it's hot enough. some people put in a wooden spoon. When it makes sizzling noises, the oil's ready too.

Gram flour, in case you didn't know is made from the wonderful chickpea.

Dear Soya Beans.
I know you've got a glamorous jet-setting lifestyle and a complete set of amino acids, blah blah blah, but tofu will only get you so far into my affections when there's hummus, falafels and pakoras in the world. Let it be shouted from the roofs and written in indelible ink on things. Chickpeas are without doubt the greatest bean ever.
Yours sincerely, etc.

Instructions

5 lumps frozen whole spinach, de-frosted, squeezed dry and roughly chopped

1½ cups gram flour

1 medium potato, finely diced

1 small onion, finely diced

1 cup plain vegan yogurt

1 cup chopped fresh coriander

2 tsp cumin seeds

1 tsp ground coriander

½ tsp ground fenugreek

1 fresh red chilli, finely chopped

½ tsp turmeric

Salt

Combine all the ingredients together. Introduce the water at the end, a little at a time, stirring it in until you have a thick batter, one that is moist but doesn't dribble off a spoon.

Taste the mix and adjust the seasonings as needed.

Take a rounded table spoonful of the mix and slide it into a wok of hot oil with another spoon. Keep adding more to the oil until there's no more space.

Leave to cook for thirty seconds or so before poking or jiggling them free of the sides and base of the wok. After another couple of minutes, turn them over. Fry for another three to four minutes or until golden brown on both sides.

Remove them with a slatted spoon and leave to stand on some kitchen roll for a minute to let the oil drain away.

Eat, devour, test for tastiness over and over again.

Falafels

Ideally, falafels should be made from brown broad beans as in the Egyptian/Lebanese version but they're hard to source in this country, so this is Israeli style. Even made with chickpeas they remain utterly fantastic. This will serve seven or eight people. Don't use any other beans to make this recipe. Some can be toxic in their raw state, so stick to these two.

   Make sure the oil completely covers the falafels when putting them in, otherwise they'll turn into oily gloop immediately. And if the oil's too hot, you'll cook the outside in thirty seconds, leaving the inside of the falafels raw, so just put in one initially to test.

   Serve with tahini, chilli sauce and salad in a pitta bread.

Instructions

500g/just under 3½ cups of dried chickpeas (or dried brown broad beans)

3 medium onions

1 red chilli

4 tsp ground cumin

4 tsp ground coriander

1 tsp turmeric

1 cup chopped fresh coriander

Salt

Soak the dried chickpeas in lots of water for at least twelve hours and up to twenty four hours.

Drain off the water and rinse then pour into a food processor bowl. You might need to divide the chickpeas into two if the bowl is small.

Quickly whizz them up until there's a roughly grainy mix and scrape out into a large mixing bowl.

Quarter three medium onions and add to the chickpeas with either one or two roughly chopped chillies depending on strength, the ground cumin, coriander, turmeric, chopped fresh coriander and salt.

Mix then re-food process the mix. You might need to divide it into three. The finer the mix, the better it sticks together, so do what you can before re-combining. Finish the mix off, if it needs it, with a hand blender.

Taste the mix and adjust for salt etc. and roll into balls or small patties, slightly flattening top and bottom and lay on plates until all the falafels are made up.

Deep fry batches in a wok with oil just hot enough to lift a scrap of bread or similar. Lift them out after five minutes when they're golden brown and drain onto kitchen towels. They can be kept warm in a pre-heated dish with some foil to cover the top.

If doubling up the quantities for a larger group of people, use one less onion than the recipe would suggest. For some reason, the mix gets too runny otherwise.

Samosas

I can't even tell you how good these are. Just make them.

Instead of making your own pastry, you could make up little triangular wraps using bought filo pastry. This is done by laying out a sheet of filo, cutting it in half lengthways, then adding a spoon or so of the mix into one of the bottom corners. Then all you do is fold the corner over onto the opposite long side and continue flipping and folding in triangles upwards until the parcel is made. It's actually very easy so just give it a go.

Instructions

2½ cups white flour

½ tsp salt

3 tbsp oil

To make the dough, combine the white flour and salt with the oil to make a crumb. Slowly add water until you have a dough. Knead for a few minutes and set aside in a covered bowl or wrap it in cling-film until needed.

1 large potato, diced

1 tsp mustard seeds

1 tbsp sunflower oil

1½ tsp ground cumin

½ tsp ground coriander

1 onion, finely chopped

1 heaped tbsp garden peas

½ red chilli, finely chopped

½ tsp turmeric

Salt and black pepper

Boil the diced potato bits until just cooked. Drain and set aside.

Fry the mustard seeds in oil until popping.

Add the ground cumin and coriander, the onion and chilli and fry on a low heat until soft.

Add the cooked diced potato, peas and turmeric and continue gently frying for a couple of minutes until the ingredients have all combined. Salt and pepper to taste.

Divide the dough into little lumps and roll each in turn into a thin circle on a floured surface. Cut in half, then take the semi-circle of dough and form a cone by bringing the two ends together after moistening the edge with water. Crimp the edge closed with your finger-tips. Hold the cone in a loose fist while you spoon in some of the mix, then seal the top, again after moistening. Crimp again.

Deep fry the little samosas briefly until golden, turning once to ensure even cooking. Just shy of a minute I reckon for the filo ones, a little longer for the pastry ones.

Scrambled Tofu

I guess this started off with me wanting to recapture the hearty breakfast quality of the scrambled eggs with tomatoes that I used to have when I was younger. Then I found I wasn't the only one wanting it. But nearly all the other recipes I read were shockingly awful. Some glimmerings of hope in a couple but to be honest, most non-vegans would be wiping their tongues clean within seconds of tasting the stuff. So here's mine with the simple added benefit of actually tasting good and not rank. As with the lasagne recipe, it's not trying to compete with real scrambled eggs but with the myriad of other scrambled tofu recipes out there.

   This will serve two people.

Instructions

1 tbsp sunflower oil

½ onion, finely chopped

1 garlic clove

1 tbsp white flour

½ cup soya milk

One 226g/8oz block fresh plain tofu, crumbled

3 medium vine tomatoes, finely chopped

1 tsp wholegrain mustard

½ tsp mixed dried herbs

10 basil leaves, torn

Salt and freshly ground black pepper

In a small thick-bottomed pan, add the oil and fry the onion and garlic on a low heat until browning.

Stir in the flour and allow to cook on for a few seconds before adding the soya milk, a little at a time.

Add the tofu, tomatoes, mustard and dried herbs and stir, still on a low heat, for three minutes.

Put slices of bread in the toaster to toast while you add the basil leaves and season to taste.

Serve on toast.

Desserts

Desserts

Ah. The most difficult thing I find with vegan cuisine is finding desserts good enough that even non-vegans will devour them and go back for seconds. This has to always be the bottom line. If they can pass that test, then you're onto a winner. Usually though, vegan desserts either look or taste like a dog's dinner, if it was full of sugar as well. The chapter won't be long but I'll try to stop your attention from wandering.

   The most useful thing to have is an ice cream maker. Once purchased, the combinations are endless and it's possible to make vegan sorbets and ice creams that are perfectly acceptable for even the most dairy obsessed person in the world. There are a few other things that are acceptable to the cream and butter loaded taste buds of the population at large too. And here some of them jolly well are.

Mint and Chocolate Chip Ice Cream

This ice cream recipe contains the basis for many others in its tender grasp.
Starting with the first five ingredients, you can add whatever your imagination can come up with. Banana, peach, strawberries... If you want to use liqueurs in the mix, bear in mind that alcohol doesn't freeze so go easy on the amounts or you'll end up with runny cold stuff slopping about in your freezer container and no ice cream to be found anywhere.

Instructions

One 349g/12oz Tetra pak firm silken tofu

¾ cup soya milk

4 tbsp sunflower oil

⅓ cup maple syrup

1 tsp vanilla essence

2 tsp peppermint essence

Green food colouring (optional)

¾ cup plain chocolate chips

Into a food processor, put the silken tofu, soya milk, oil, maple syrup, the vanilla essence and peppermint and the green food colouring if you're using it.

Whizz up.

Pour into a bowl and mix in the chocolate chips.

Turn into ice cream using a magical ice cream maker.

If you've only got a freezer, then put the mix into a suitable container and put in the freezer, stirring every half hour or so as the mixture freezes. This will stop the worst of the ice crystals forming.

Peach and Marzipan Tarte Tatin

Ever since I was little, marzipan has been the sweet highlight of Christmas dinner. It's a wonderful invention. Put with peaches and puff pastry...

Instructions

3 tbsp margarine

½ cup brown sugar

3 tbsp apricot high fruit conserve

1 tbsp fresh lemon juice

5 ripe peaches

One 500g/17oz or somewhere near it block frozen puff pastry, defrosted

Half a 454g/1lb block good quality egg-free marzipan

In an eight inch tarte tatin pan, high sided skillet or cast iron frying pan, heat up the margarine and sugar over a low heat for about six minutes until the mixture turns golden brown and begins to bubble. Heat the apricot conserve and lemon juice separately with a tablespoon of water and when bubbling, add in to the caramel and stir until the melted sugar accepts the inevitable.

Plunge the peaches in boiling water for two minutes then ease off their skins. Cut them in half, then into slices, de-stoning as you go. Closely line them in the tarte tatin pan in a pleasing and ergonomical use of the space available.

On a low heat, let the peaches cook with the caramel for about twenty minutes until softening and giving off their juices.

Allow to cool for ten minutes, then break or cut the marzipan into small chunks and lay them in amongst the dips of the peaches.

Roll out the puff pastry and trim so it's circular and an inch wider than the rim of the tarte tatin pan.

Lay over the peaches and ease the edges of the puff pastry down between the pan and the edges of the peaches to form a seal, cutting a vent hole in the top.

Put in a pre-heated 200ºC oven for about half an hour or at least until the puff pastry has risen and turned golden brown.

Take out of the oven and leave to stand for ten minutes then slip a knife round the edge of the puff pastry to loosen the tarte sides then find a plate larger than the pan to place over the puff pastry top.

Upturn the pan and lift slowly away from the plate. Your mound of molten marzipan and caramelised goodness awaits.

Chocolate Brownies

Instructions

½ cup margarine

1 cup sugar

3 tbsp oil

One 349g/12oz Tetra pak firm silken tofu

⅓ cup cocoa

1 tsp vanilla extract

1⅓ cups plain flour

2 tsp baking powder

½ cup chopped dates

2 cups chocolate chips

Combine the margarine, sugar and oil in a food processor before adding the silken tofu, cocoa and vanilla extract and processing again.

Turn out into a mixing bowl and sift in the flour and baking powder, gently folding them in until combined.

Stir in the dates and chocolate chips before putting in a baking parchment fitted 9 inch square baking tin.

Bake at 180ºC for thirty minutes. The top of the cake should spring back when pressed for readiness.

Remove from the oven and allow to cool a little before turning out onto a cooling rack.

Rich Fruit Cake

This is a dense Christmas style cake and the sort I absolutely adore. I think the technique of cooking it was originally part Delia-inspired. It's hard not to be as she's pretty much unbeatable on making cakes.

  Chocolate aside, this is an overall vegan favourite.

Instructions

4½ cups mixed vine fruit

½ cup cherries

½ cup dried chopped figs

½ cup dried chopped dates

½ cup brandy

Zest and juice 1 orange

1 cup margarine

1 cup dark Muscavado sugar

2¾ cups self raising flour

¾ cup soya flour

¼ tsp salt

2 tsp mixed spice

1 tbsp blackstrap molasses

Just over ½ cup water

½ cup flaked almonds

⅓ cup broken Macadamia nuts

Put all the fruit into a bowl. Add the brandy and orange zest and juice, cover and allow to soak overnight.

Cream the margarine and sugar in a large bowl with either a brisk fork or a very brisk whisk before sieving in the flours, salt and mixed spice.

Fold the flour into the creamed mixture gently. Don't over-stir. It knocks all the air out of the mix and vegan cakes need all the help they can get.

Thin the molasses in the water and gently fold into the cake mix with the nuts.

Line the base of a nine inch cake tin with a double thickness of baking parchment and do the same around the sides, leaving two inches of paper above the lip of the tin to allow for the hopefully expanding cake.

Wrap the outside of the tin with doubled up brown paper or newspaper and tie with string. This is to disguise the cake should enemy cakes infiltrate the oven.

Carefully spoon in the mixture, smoothing off the top with the back of a spoon.

Cover with a double layer of baking parchment and cook in the middle of a 140°C oven for a good three hours until a skewer comes out of the centre pretty clean.

Allow to cool in the tin for half an hour before turning it out onto a cooling rack. When cool, store in an air-tight tin.

Until you use the cake, periodically feed the cake with more brandy by skewering small holes into the cake and drizzling a teaspoon or so of the stuff over the top.

Mayan Chocolate Cake

This makes a rich and spicy cake, a little smaller than normal, probably serving six people.

Instructions

½ cup white spelt flour

1 cup ground almonds

½ cup cocoa

2 tsp baking powder

½ cup margarine

½ cup brown sugar

1 tsp vanilla essence

1 tsp orange essence

4 tsp sweet mixed spice

½ tsp cayenne pepper

Zest 2 oranges

¾ cup soya milk

70g/2½ oz dark chocolate

1 tbsp margarine

Zest 1 orange

Put the flour, almonds, cocoa and baking powder in a bowl and mix together thoroughly.

In a separate bowl, cream together the rest of the ingredients apart from the soya milk.

Combine until you have a stiff chocolate coloured dough.

Gradually stir in the soya milk and mix thoroughly.

Scrape out into a greased and lined six inch cake tin and place in a pre-heated 160ºC oven for thirty five to forty minutes.

Remove from the oven and allow to stand for five minutes before turning out onto a cooling rack.

When cool, melt the chocolate, orange zest and margarine in a bowl above simmering water and spoon onto the cake.

Allow to set before serving.

Princess Noo's Macaroon Slice

A friend of mine, Nicky Noo, who'll happily make cakes to celebrate sunny days, new socks and waking up, not only invented the previous cake but made me this one as my birthday cake this year. It's not often I have a memorable cake these days, but this was just sublime. And unbelievably, it's completely gluten-free.

Instructions

2 ⅓ cups roughly chopped dates

1½ cups water

1½ cups finely ground almonds

1½ cups dessicated coconut

4 heaped tsp arrowroot

2 tbsp brown sugar

2½ tsp baking powder

4 tbsp date syrup

½ cup sunflower oil

½ tsp vanilla essence

Zest 1 lemon

1 tbsp fresh lemon juice

Put the dates and water into a pan and simmer for five minutes covered on a low heat until the dates are turning a little mushy. Pushing down on the date pulp a little, pour off the liquid into a jug. Reserve. Slightly mash the dates before allowing both the dates and date water to cool slightly.

Combine all the dry ingredients in a bowl and mix together.

Stir the date syrup into the oil, add the vanilla essence, then pour into the bowl with the dry ingredients and mix thoroughly.

Prepare a nine inch cake tin or similar by greasing and lining with baking parchment before scraping the dates in and spreading smoothly across the base.

Put the lemon zest and juice into the reserved date water and then pour into the prepared cake mix and stir. The mixture should be moist but not runny, but if it feels a little too dry, add a little more water.

Pour the mix over the mashed dates immediately and smooth off the top with the back of a spoon.

Cover with foil and put in an 170º C oven for about half an hour before removing the foil and cooking for a further quarter of an hour uncovered.

Remove from oven and allow to cool slightly before upturning the tin onto a chopping board and allowing to cool.

Dust with dessicated coconut across the surface for added pizzazz and pose and other Ps.

Panforte Nero

Panforte Nero is an extremely rich Italian cake/slice from Sienna, needing the restraint of thin slices rather than thick wedges or else the sugar rush might tip you into la la land.

   This cake would normally have bee's puke* in it rather than maple syrup. So if you're a vegan-who-has-honey type of person then adjust your jars according to the desire for said insect up-chuck*.

Gross, I know, but I can't honey-coat the truth any longer.

Instructions

100g/3½ oz plain chocolate

1 cup white flour

1 tsp ground cinnamon

¼ tsp ground allspice

¾ tsp ginger

½ tsp black pepper

2½ cups almonds, lightly toasted and chopped

1 cup chopped mixed peel

⅔ cup light brown sugar

⅓ cup maple syrup

Set the chocolate to melt over simmering water.

Meanwhile, mix the flour, spices, almonds and chopped mixed peel together in a bowl.

When the chocolate has melted, take off the heat and set aside.

Put the sugar and maple syrup into a small pan and bring to the boil over a medium heat. Now either use a cooking thermometer to determine when the mixture is at soft ball stage, at around 118ºC/235ºF, or drop a little into a small dish of cold water where it should solidify but still stay soft. It all happens quicker than you might think so be ready.

Immediately take off the heat and stir into the dry mix together with the melted chocolate. The mixture will immediately start to thicken so do it quickly.

Scrape out into a greased, lined seven inch spring-form baking tin and smooth out the top as much as possible.

Place in a 150ºC oven and bake for about forty minutes. The top should be slightly cracking.

Allow to cool for half an hour before loosening the edge of the cake with a knife and lifting out of the tin.

Remove the base of the tin and allow to fully cool.

Sprinkle with icing sugar and serve.

Millionaire's Shortbread

I've been trying for years to get a vegan version of this to work. I think I've cracked it. This was my all time favourite cake when I was little so it's nice to have it back in the repertoire while I've still got all my own teeth. This won't help to keep them though, I'm afraid. It's called millionaire's shortbread because millionaires like caramel slices. They can't get enough of the stuff.

Instructions

6 tbsp caster sugar

⅔ cup margarine

2 cups plain flour

2 tbsp coconut oil

1 tbsp vegan margarine

1 cup brown sugar

½ cup vegan soya cream

2 tbsp arrowroot

200g/7oz dark chocolate

1 tsp sunflower oil

Put the sugar and margarine in a bowl and cream together with a wooden spoon.

Stir in the flour until you have a crumbly mix. Try not to over-do.

Press into a lined nine inch baking tray, and put in 170ºC pre-heated oven for around half an hour, until it's pale yet golden in colour.

Remove from the oven and allow to cool.

Put the coconut oil, margarine, sugar and soya cream into a small pan and heat on a high heat, stirring constantly. When the mix starts to boil, continue stirring for another three minutes before taking off the heat.

When the bubbles have subsided, add in the arrowroot and stir in until dissolved.

Pour immediately over the shortbread base, smoothing off the surface and allow to set.

When cool, break up the chocolate into a glass bowl with the sunflower oil and melt over simmering water until melted.

Pour over the top of the caramel and smooth out with the back of a spoon.

When half set, score where you want the cuts to be so that slicing will be easier.

Cut and eat in a Jacuzzi with a glass of champagne and a sexy other.

Walnut Biscotti

Hurray! A sugar-free, margarine-free recipe. A bit of a classy Italian one, this, to be nibbled at with an expresso of course.

Instructions

3 cups plain flour

1 tbsp baking powder

¼ tsp salt

1 cup walnuts, ground

½ cup sunflower oil

½ cup maple syrup

1½ tsp vanilla extract

2 tsp almond extract

Sift the flour, baking powder and salt through a sieve into a mixing bowl.

Add the ground walnuts.

In a jug, mix the oil, maple syrup, vanilla extract and almond extract together.

Slowly mix into the dry ingredients until combined. You should have a firm mix, not at all runny. If it is, add a bit more flour.

Divide the mix in half and form two logs about two and a half inches wide on a tray covered with baking parchment.

Bake for thirty minutes at 150°C then remove from the oven and allow to cool slightly.

Cut diagonally into half inch thick slices and return the slices separated and spread on the baking tray to the oven for a further fifteen minutes. Job done.

If you so desire it, when the biscotti is fully cooled, melt a bar of plain chocolate with a tablespoon of sunflower oil and dip each slice half into the melted chocolate. Allow to set before eating.

Mexican Wedding Biscuits

1 cup pecans

1 cup decent vegan margarine, if that exists

½ cup powdered sugar

1 ½ tsp real vanilla essence

2 cup plain flour

½ tsp cinnamon

¼ tsp of salt

Instructions

Lightly roast the pecans and then lightly grind in a food processor. Don't turn it to paste though. Way too far.

Mix the margarine, sugar and vanilla essence together with a hand whisk until light and fluffy. Fold in the nuts, flour, cinnamon and salt until it forms a dough. The less fiddling the better so don't over-do it.

Allow the dough to chill before rolling into small walnut sized balls and place on a baking parchment-covered tray.

Bake for quarter of an hour in a 160°C oven before cooling on a wire rack.

Dust with more powdered sugar and serve.

About the Author

A vegan for nineteen years, Andy has cooked professionally for seven years. His previous attempts were sadly amateurish and not worthy of note. He has tried to be funny since little and feels that mixing cooking and New Age comedy together was a necessary and life defining experience and definitely a really good idea.

As an Aquarian Fire-pony/Cosmic Monkey, of course Andy wasn't ever going to believe in astrology, or anything else either. It's obvious to anyone. His cynicism was pre-destined by the stars. He's had about as much choice in the matter as deciding his eye colour (kind of blue, kind of grey).

He lives and works in Somerset where he has a great time enjoying the flat, featureless landscape and the perpetual mist and rain.